PROJECT MANAGEMENT:
THE BLACK EXPERIENCE

Survival Guide for the African-American Project Manager

ERIC D. PANNELL, MBA, PMP

For my family who supports me daily (Tara, Jeremiah, Jadon, & Audrey)

For my parents, who think I'm great no matter what.

CONTENTS

PREFACE

This book is dedicated to my mother, Connie; my father Melvin; and my sister Necy; additionally to the whole Brooks and Pannell family. You have molded me into the man that I am today and always inspired me to dream big dreams. From the bottom of my heart, I just want to thank you for always being there and encouraging me.

This book is also dedicated to my city, Bluefield, West Virginia. So many memories going to church, playing at the playground, school teachers, and it's way too many people to name so I'm doing my best here to lump everything into one. Living here in Charlotte, North Carolina, people are always surprised to learn that I'm from West Virginia obviously because I'm black. Bluefield you are my foundation and the reason I'm the person that I am. It would be easy for me to wish I grew up in a big city, but I'm proud to say I'm from Bluefield. I love you all. This is for you!

Last, but certainly not least, this book is dedicated to my wife, Sekayi. I want to thank you for being by my side throughout my journey writing this book and my other crazy endeavors. It's not easy being married to a high-demanding dreamer. If I could give you the truth serum you would let the world know that many nights you wanted to kill me because of my crazy ideas and focus. But through it all, you express it with love. To the best kids a man could have Jeremiah and Jadon, thank you for supporting me even when you have no idea what it is I'm doing. I hope for you both this sets the example that ordinary people can dream and do big things. I love you all!

INTRODUCTION

While many of you spent every Friday as a kid watching the Thank God its Friday (TGIF) shows, coming off a long week of school. I looked forward to Friday's because my mother and father had a collection of black history books to teach me various important lessons from the past. It was not only my opportunity to bond with my parents but learn about African-American history. Being raised in West Virginia, I'm sure you can imagine that I wasn't getting the "real" black history message in school. There has always been a message stuck in my mind back then from my parents that still speaks loudly in my head, "when it comes to being black, you have to be two times better."

It wasn't until later in life as an adult that message truly meant anything meaningful to me. The main reason why is because I had plenty of white friends back then and still do to this day and the only competing I was doing back then was on the basketball court. I had no idea that the time that they were preparing me for was in the game of life and corporate America. I graduated high school, got a scholarship to play basketball at Bluefield State College. Like many other college students, I didn't have a plan for want I wanted to do coming out of college. There was a direct plan to become an engineer, accountant, and certainly not an attorney. I had the urge to be an entrepreneur, but I never fully took the time to map out what I wanted to do. Before you know it I'm walking across the stage in May of 2002, and my bags were packed heading down the Charlotte, North Carolina.

I started writing this book, at least in my mind, about a year into starting my Project Management experience, about 14 years ago. I live in Charlotte, NC and have been here now for about 16 years. For the past 14 years, I have been running all types of projects in the technology space, and for about 11 of those has been in the Fortune 500 arena.

I started out as a Technical Recruiter where I would recruit Project Managers and other technical resources. My role consisted of interviewing a pool of candidates and when a job that matched their skill-set I would then submit them for an opening with one of the large companies we worked with. At that time I was making around $40,000 per year, not including commission. I quickly started to notice the difference between my salary and the Project Managers I placed for these jobs. They were making $50+ per hour, in some cases, $80 per hour depended upon the complexity of the project skill-set.

I never had the desire to be a Project Manager, but it was at that moment I realized that if I wanted to make that kind of money I needed to do a quick makeover. So, I started to quickly network with experienced Project Managers, updated my resume, and literally went on hundreds of interviews. I went on what seems like hundreds of interviews, rejection after rejection. Nothing was going to keep me away from getting this money and becoming a PM, so giving up wasn't an option.

Until one day, I went on an interview that I felt I nailed, and immediately got the call back hearing on the other end. "Eric, the manager just called us back, he really liked your interview and wants to hire you!" I was driving and had to pull over on the side of the road. I, of course, said yes, and at that moment I went from making $19 per hour to $42 per hour. I called my mom crying with joy, she starts crying, and it was literally at that time at the top of my list of greatest achievements.

Even though my mom and dad always taught me about black history, I was certainly not prepared to face the African-American experience in corporate America. My sole goal was to reach six figures in annual income and I completely disregarded the type of role and definitely didn't research the impacts of being an African-American IT Project Manager. I just knew that I didn't want to work on the frontline in a call center or a support role on the phone talking to customers.

Throughout my career as a black Project Manager, there has been many ups and downs, from increasing pay, a higher level of responsibility, to layoffs, and being held back from roles. I wouldn't change that experience for the world as it has allowed me to acquire the knowledge to share with other aspiring African-American Project Managers.

For many years Corporate America earned the perception as a place for housing only white men in the navy blue suit with firm handshakes. It wasn't until 1987 until, when Dr. Clifton R. Wharton, Jr, became the first Black CEO of a Fortune 500 company, this image shifted. This one critical occurrence put the spotlight on diversity in Corporate America as a whole throughout companies, and even in executive level positions.

Of course, diversity in the corporate workplace has gotten much better but there is still a very long gap that we must close together (both black and white). It's no secret that African-Americans are severely underrepresented in corporate America---in 2011, we held only 6.7 percent of the management jobs.

The data that has been collected supports the understanding for African-Americans entering the workplace that the hardest challenge isn't just getting the job. The true challenge is surviving the corporate landscape as an

African-American. In order to do this, you must understand the survival tools you must equip yourself with on a daily basis.

Being an African-American in the workplace comes at a great cost, more than just feeling less confident or alone. In particular, black professionals have to be very careful to show feelings of conviviality and pleasantness, even—especially—in response to racial issues. They felt that emotions of anger, frustration, and annoyance were discouraged, even when the work in settings where these emotions were generally welcomed in certain contexts.

Being an African-American in the Project Management world displays an even wider gap between blacks and our fellow white team members. The reality is throughout my career as a Project Manager working in corporate America I have been mostly the only African-American or one of a few. Many times when you're just appreciative to have your ideal job, we start to lose sight of what's taking place around you. You miss the fact that there is hiring taking place around you but then you start to realize not only are African-Americans getting interviews and definitely not getting hired. You start to ask yourself, "why is that"?

Throughout the as an African-American in corporate America, it's important that we adapt but also keep your identity to reach your optimal level of production. There are many issues that come with the survival of being black in the workplace… many will work longer hours to fit in, change their voice or posture in the presence of their white counterparts, and many other tactics.

This book stems from my many years of experience as an African-American IT Project Manager working at Fortune 500 companies. African-Americans are landing project management jobs, but facing the overwhelming isolation in the workplace across the country. My primary goal in writing this book is to raise the awareness of this glaring issue and to share real-life experiences to help those entering the project management space with some key tips and tools. You will read about some personal experiences of not only myself but many other African-American Project Managers across the country that I have personal talked with adding validity to this issue. There's no reason why the future of project management can be more balanced with the talent pool of both whites and blacks in all position levels.

This book is not intended to change the perception that blacks have towards white people, certainly not negatively. I have many close friends that are white, love them dearly, and that will never change. I want this book to shed the light on the inequalities that exist for "human beings" that happen to be black. The American Dream of you go to college, get a good job, start a family, and live a happy life is not equal for everyone today. The numbers support that this dream is truer for whites than blacks. My personal experiences as a Project Manager support this as well.

The average salary for a low-to-mid level Project Manager $78,000 to $94,000 and the average for a Senior Project Manager is between $100,000 to $150,000+ per year. For the middle-class worker in the state of North Carolina that $20,000 to $70,000 higher if you successfully land one of those jobs. People of color are highly represented in call center jobs, processors, and other low-to-mid-tier roles. But there is a significant gap with lucrative jobs in tech for developers and especially project management. Many studies show that far too many African-Americans are either not getting jobs or forced to leave due to unfair practices:

Nearly one-quarter of underrepresented men and women of color experienced stereotyping, twice the rate of white and Asian men and women.

Nearly one-third of underrepresented women of color were passed over for promotion, more than any other group.

Men from underrepresented groups, such as African-Americans, Latinos and Native Americans, were most likely to leave due to unfairness (40%).

Underrepresented women of color were significantly more likely to cite unfairness as reasons for leaving than white and Asian women (36% versus 28%).

It wasn't until I started my career as a Project Manager that I realized this and was forced to face these issues head-on. Surviving as an African-American in tech and as a Project Manager has more to do than just doing your job well. There are many other aspects of the job and corporate America that you will have to master that our fellow white workers can't relate to but can help in many ways. I hope this book helps the journey of the African-American Project Manager and provides some positive insight into your experience. Regardless how many challenges you face always remember to be professional, be yourself, and remember to embrace being black. Don't run from it.

PROJECT MANAGEMENT:
THE BLACK EXPERIENCE

CHAPTER 1

The Challenge for Minorities in Corporate America

"When life gets harder, challenge yourself to be stronger."

It's important to highlight and illustrate the challenges African-Americans face in corporate America. We will take a deeper dive into the Project Management aspect in the coming chapters, but it's important to understand the high-level challenges to see how they impact the niche space of the project management world.

More African-Americans have entered into corporate America than at any other time in the nation's history. Even with this appealing growth and access, research shows that African-Americans continue to be challenged with racism and disparate treatments, which presents a major challenge in their career development.

As a kid, my father would pull out his collection of Black History books teaching me all the things that I never learned going through all levels of school.

There was always one key saying that he instilled in me that I never forgot, "you have to show that you're two times better than whites". He used this first in the context of playing sports, but I later found out that this also was very true throughout my corporate and everyday life as well. I walk into the corporate landscape with this saying from my dad literally tattooed on my brain whenever I'm presented with adversity and challenges.

Education is a key fundamental element in the progression of anyone's career. There are many discussions and debates as to whether the Historical Black College or University (HBCU) experience truly prepares young African-Americans for the "real-world" of corporate America. Most of their four year experience is that of other fellow African-Americans, which provides all the trust and confidence they need to succeed in their endeavors. Unfortunately, this experience is not the reality of what they will face in their corporate experience for many years down the road.

Growing up in Bluefield, WV as an African-American male presented a lot of challenges but it also prepared me for me corporate experience once I moved to Charlotte, NC. I can't tell you how many times that both blacks and whites are surprised to hear that I'm from West Virginia. The looks on their face are priceless.

If you're an African-American looking for a nice six figure salary to support the lifestyle you desire and take care of your family you must master being black in corporate America. The reality is African-Americans make up approximately twelve percent of the workforce, of that twelve percent; only approximately twenty-seven percent are college graduates. According to a corporate diversity survey by the office of Senator Bob Menendez, black men and women account for only 4.7 percent of executive team members in the Fortunate 100.

When diversity is represented in executive level positions, that momentum of leadership trickles down and impacts the corporation as a whole. Even though knowing this, it still remains that opportunities for upper-level management for African-Americans just aren't there. For various reasons, the numbers don't support blacks being successfully placed in these positions. Studies show that blacks in society and corporate America are viewed as seemingly angry, intimidating, incapable of performing well in their role, or even worse "fitting in". According to Fortune, Black executives often have to play the role of "happy warrior," mastering the art of being exceptional but not frightening.

Circling back to what my parents always told me, "your good enough isn't enough and you have to be two times better". I've learned through the years that those phrases alone aren't good enough to allow you to survive the African-American experience in corporate America. In fact, there are four key areas that will be highlighted in this book you must add to your survival kit:

1. Your personal and cultural identity will influence your career development as an African-American.
2. Internal and external resources are vital to the growth of the African-American corporate American development experience.
3. Constraints you MUST overcome as an African-American man that white men or African-American women don't normally experience.
4. Utilizing tips, tools, and strategies to enhance your survival as an African-American to enhance your career development.

You will take a deeper dive into these 4 areas as they will be vital to the development of your experience as an African-American IT Project Manager. Transitioning or getting started as a Project Manager for many isn't an easy task, especially for African-Americans. But once you're in, you will quickly realize that there aren't many of us there and definitely not in leadership positions. You will have the experience of being the only "one" in virtual and physical conference meetings.

If you're currently in the project management space now… how do you handle that? How does that make you feel? If you're getting started in project management these are issues you will have to face and questions you need to be prepared to answer for yourself. How do you go about being who you truly are but still remaining professional in the eyes of other white professionals? Through my research I have discovered that there are many African-American and minority Project Managers in general are struggling with these issues.

In the next chapter, we are going to talk about the challenges of landing your first project management role, especially as an African-American. You will see the glaring challenges and some tools you can utilize as you progress or just now getting started

CHAPTER 2

Breaking in as an African-American

"Frontline love. It is our one hope for breaking down barriers and for restoring the sense of community, of caring for one another, that our decadent, impersonalized culture has sucked out of us." – Charles Colson

For anyone, not just African-Americans, landing your first project management job can be very difficult and challenging. There is not a direct path to a Project Manager job like there is for engineers, accountants, doctors, attorneys, and others. In most cases these jobs are made available to internal employees with years of on-the-job experience, then they get the proper training to transition into the project management role.

Surviving as an African-American Project Manager is challenging enough but trying to land your first project management job as an African-American is even harder. But I assure you it's not impossible and later in this chapter I'm going to show you how if you're reading this as an aspiring Project Manager.

Let's first break down why it's difficult to break into the project management role then transition into some key tips and strategies to make it happen. Project work is generally highly visible initiatives that help enhance the abilities of a company to better serve their external and internal (employees, managers, etc.) customers. So if you work for a financial services firm there could be projects put in place to enhance the way their customers perform online transactions or reduce the number of times a customer needs to call into the call center to requests transactions. Even more highly visible…. The federal government is cracking the whip on the banks across the country. So there are regulatory projects which are extremely highly visible that more seasoned Project Managers will need to lead. As you can see, it makes sense that hiring a flurry of entry-level Project Managers is very difficult and just doesn't make much "business" sense for this to happen.

As I mentioned earlier, landing your first project management job can be extremely challenging but not impossible. I know this for sure because I walked this journey and fourteen years later here I am writing this book sharing the strategies for you to follow my path or even exceed my experiences. Prior to landing my first project management role, my education consisted of Bachelors of Science (B.S.) in Business Administration, specializing in Marketing and Management. My roles consisted of working for a rental car company, advertising sales, answering the phone in a call center, and technical recruiter.

When I worked as a technical recruiter, recruiting Project Managers to fill open positions with companies across the U.S. that changed me. I made a modest $40,000 per year but every day I talked to Project Managers making in the upper $100K+ range. But I also noticed that not many of them where African-American like myself, so that left me with a lot of questions. One, why aren't there many Project Managers that I'm talking to that look like me?

20

The other is, how can I get in as an African-American Project Manager when there seems so much of a shortage to fill these positions? But I have a very determined mindset so there was nothing that's going to stop me from finding out. Below I'm going to show you the 5 key strategies I figured out how to land my first project management job.

5 Key Strategies to Land Your First Project Management Job

After landing my first project management job, I later went on the get a Masters in Project Management and obtain the highest certification the Project Management Professional (PMP). But before all of that, I was at square one with a hope and a dream. I'm going to give you the blueprint now, but through a long period of trial-and-error, I develop five key strategies that helped me land my first project management gig.

1 - TAKE INVENTORY OF YOUR SKILLS

Although your current role may not directly match to that of a Project Manager, there are certain skills that you utilize daily that are in line with project management work. The skills of a Project Manager are exceptional skills in the areas of organizational, communication, listening, leadership, and relationship building. In all of my roles, I worked on "outside projects" that were outside my primary role as a salesman or call center rep. Naturally, I got comfortable talking to people, leading initiatives, communicating, just about everything the project management role requires. I'm also fully aware that my highest quality is that I'm an exceptional relationship builder and connect with people.

Your first step is to take a sheet of paper out and write down all of the skills you utilize in your current role that matches up with that of a seasoned Project Manager. No matter what your role is, there are things that you do inside of work or maybe even outside of work in which you use these skills often. Just as I recognize my highest quality as relationship building, you need to be certain that you know what you highest quality is. Are you a great communicator? Are you an exceptional planner? Do people see you as a leader? Don't skip this exercise because it is extremely important for you to know.

If you find this exercise difficult because you currently don't perform any of these activities outside your current job then now is the time to start. When "special project" requests come up within your team, then you need to be the first to nominate yourself. Get in the habit of performing these skills because they will be critical as you start to update your resume.

Finally, you want to take what you've written down on your sheet of paper, and start to update your resume to reflect the project work that you've done. While updating your resume alone will not solely land you your first project management gig, it is a vital beginning step. Go through each of your roles and start to highlight where you have led meetings, led a group of people, improved a process, or enhanced the way something works within your company. These are all attractive activities to catch a recruiter's eye as well as the decision-maker for various project management opportunities.

Once you've updated your resume share it with someone close to you, colleague, mentor (if you have one) or a seasoned advocate of your career. This is important because they know you best and can give you immediate feedback on your updates. Both negative and positive feedback is good here at this stage because you want it to be polished up before you put it out in front of recruiters and managers.

2 – NETWORKING (ONLINE & OFFLINE)

Who you know and who knows you are extremely vital not just to land a project management job but to virtually land any attractive job. Networking is vital to land the hidden job or transition into an attractive job not directly in line with your current role. Unfortunately, research shows that African-Americans struggle when it comes to networking and landing the hidden roles. In a new study published by the Russell Sage Foundation, Nancy DiTomaso, a professor of organization management at Rutgers University, says "hidden" forms of racial inequality tied to seemingly innocuous things like networking are holding black job-seekers back".

When I first started out making my transition into the project management world, Google and LinkedIn became my go-to tools. I knew where every project management event was taking place in Charlotte and I made sure I was connected to a good group of Project Managers locally and nationally. This is the reason why this strategy is called networking (online and offline). With the technology that's provided to us today, there should never be a reason you don't know where Project Managers are meeting and you should be able to easily fill up a list of Project Managers to network and connect with. Now we have Meetup.com which has Project Management meetup meetings happening all across the country.

As you start to network with other Project Managers it's important that you get your mindset together so that you aren't wasting people's time. What is your main goal? Your main goal is to land a project management job. But when you're networking this is not your main goal. Your main goal while networking is to build a relationship first, soak up as much industry knowledge as possible, learn who they know, which will lead you to your main goal of landing a project management job.

Project Managers use certain skills that we discussed earlier, they use certain lingo, and they use certain methodologies and tools to manage certain projects. Even though you don't have the direct experience you will want to start to learn these things and get them baked into your mind. As you start to interview which we will discuss later, these things will come up from recruiters testing to understand your knowledge and understanding. There are certain tools like SharePoint, PowerPoint, MS Project, Excel, that Project Manager's use you can learn on teaching sites like www.udemy.com. Jump ahead and learn these skills now and put them in your knowledge toolbox.

I started out first by making it clearly aware and transparent to people that I was desperate for a project management job and that was a huge mistake in the beginning. Regardless if I met someone face-to-face or online, I started with:

"Hi my name is Eric Pannell, and I noticed you have years of experience as a Project Manager. Would love to get 10-15 minutes of your time to learn more about your experience as a Project Manager."

If they ask why I then share that I'm making the transition and really intrigued by your experience. Mastering the skill of networking is all about building the person up that you want to connect with (i.e. need something from). Make it all about them first, then they will be more than happy to talk with you.

It's very obvious that as an African-American male, I naturally connected and reached out to them first. The key reason is that they've successfully made the transition to the "other" side and leveraging their experience not only gives the knowledge but confidence as well.

As a take away to the section, you must make networking a key element to not only land your first project management job. But it will also be critical once you start to excel in your role and looking to advance your career. Do you still doubt how vital networking is for your career? A study done in 2009 stated that "Ninety-nine percent of a recruiter's interviewees received seventy percent of the jobs they held over their lifetimes with the extra help of friends or family members." These are the types of contacts that could give you the inside information, their influence, or offer you opportunities for promotions not public to others.

If you don't already, go now and set up a LinkedIn and Meetup account. This where your online and offline networking journey will start. Start to analyze how Project Managers set their profiles up. Nice professional profile picture, clearly states their title, and experience within the project management space. The next section will be brief, but you will learn why getting a mentor is critical to your success of not only landing your first project management job but enhancing your career.

3 – GET A MENTOR

The output of networking in most cases naturally you will develop a mentor, someone who will take you under their wing to guide you to your first project management role. I took networking very serious, but I also viewed getting a mentor even more critical. Having a seasoned Project Manager as your mentor is critical because as you start to update your resume and interview they can guide you through each step of your journey.

While networking through LinkedIn I developed a relationship over time with my mentor who still mentors me even today. All the mistakes that I would have made on my own, he accelerated my journey by giving me the blueprint of what to do and what not to do. Which is what I'm sharing with you know through this book.

It's highly likely that the first person you connect with will not become your mentor, as that didn't happen for me. I received a lot of ignored messages, a ton of phone calls there weren't returned, and a lot of flat out no's. But I knew what my goal was which was to land my first project management job and I never gave up. I'm not telling you this to scare you but you're going to have to develop a thick skin to master networking and securing a mentor. People are most focused on their goals and for the most part, could care less what goals you're trying to accomplish.

4 – BUILD RELATIONSHIPS WITH TECH RECRUITERS

Project Management is a very contract driven industry, which has made technical recruiting a vital part of hiring Project Managers. Instead of hiring a Project Manager full-time making them salaried employees (401k, health/medical, etc.), companies turn to contract Project Managers who get paid hourly (no benefits) to work for a certain period of time (6, 12, or 18 months). Companies normally use recruiting firms all across the country to bring them a pool of candidates to hire from. Technical recruiters get paid a modest salary, but they make the bulk of their money through commissions by successfully placing candidates. So they spend most of their days interviewing potential candidates, and "building relationships".

There are a couple of ways to get the relationship building process going with technical recruiters. They are sharks hunting on every job board hunting for candidates, Monster, CareerBuilder, Indeed, LinkedIn you name it. Once you upload your resume to any of these jobs boards you will start to receive a flurry of phone calls. Maybe not initially for a particular role but they would like to understand your skill set compared to your resume and the types of roles you're looking for. In the beginning, you may not be able to answer all of their questions like "Do you want to work on the business or tech side", but you will over time. They will also ask you, "are you interested in a contract or full-time roles"? Starting out you will likely get more offers as a contractor because of the lack of experience, etc.

Here are the pros and cons of being a contractor Project Manager:

Pros:

You will be more likely to land your first project management gig, you will get paid a higher wage by the hour, and have a quick opportunity to increase your wage through new contracts. When you produce good work as a contractor, technical recruiters will be more inclined to promote you to available opportunities.

Cons:

You will have to find your own benefits, companies can lay off contractors much easier than salaried employees, and of course, it's not as stable. If you have any kind of debt issues, or your family is heavily dependent upon your income, then you will want to think deeply about becoming a contract worker.

For this section, I want to focus squarely on the importance of building relationships with Technical Recruiters. As you start to get those calls you want to know everything it is to know about the recruiters:

- Remember their names (of course)

- What firm are they with?

- Who is their top client (the company they are recruiting for)

- What roles the recruit normally works with

- How long have they been a technical recruiter

- Do you normally see roles that fit your skillset

- Give them permission to call or email you anytime about opportunities

- Ask them is it ok to call and check in with them.

Do this with every recruiter you talk to and before you know it you will have twenty to thirty recruiters who know you and have you at the top of the mind when open opportunities come up. A lot of time the technical recruiting companies will have local events, make sure you're there. Offer to bring refer other people you know that may be a good fit. Even if you land a full-time job you should always keep a good relationship with recruiters because in today's climate there is a lack of stability for jobs. The average person today stays with their current role just under five years, that's a total difference with our parents worked thirty plus years at the same job.

Building solid relationships is your gateway to immediately landing your first project management job because they are frontline with the hiring managers. Much greater change landing a job through one of their opportunities as opposed to submitting your resume initially on one of the popular job boards. Remember in the beginning you're focused on gaining direct project management experience, and of course, increasing your salary in most cases.

So far we've talked about understanding your skills, the importance of networking, getting a mentor, and building solid relationships with technical recruiters. In the next section is when the previous steps start to pay off and your activity level starts to pick up. You're going to learn what to get out of your interviews and how to use the jobs you didn't get to propel you to landing your first project management role.

5 – START INTERVIEWING

Getting interviews is half the battle, but successfully interviewing is the other half which ultimately gets you the job. In this section, you will learn why there isn't such thing as a bad interview, how you learn from them, make the next one better, and some interviewing tips to get you the job.

As you start to build relationships with technical recruiters you will start to get various request for interviews. These are interviews in which you will have a phone or face-to-face interview with the hiring manager of a particular company. The more you interview, the more you learn period. Before I landed my first Project Management role I probably interviewed twenty plus times. After you go through each interview a few things will start to happen:

- Develop more confidence

- Get used to project management based questions

- Learn the questions you answer well

- Learn the question you struggle and need to work on

- Learn more about the project lingo and terms

- Learn more about the project tools

- Learn how to clearly speak about your skills and experience.

Each interview gives you an opportunity to audition yourself as the ideal candidate for a particular role. Interviewing does come with some struggles and challenges. If you currently work a nine-to-five job, you're going to have to find time to work your interviews in. From phone interviews, face-to-face, or even Skype. You have to find a way to figure it out, but never turn an interview down as you can see they are valuable to learn.

Getting a project management job is not as easy as just submitting your resume and waiting for someone to call you back. Because of the attractiveness of the role, it's a highly competitive industry and one that lacks the balanced presence of African-Americans. It's important to understand that not only is it difficult to land the job in general but there are additional challenges that come with being an aspiring African-American Project Manager.

CHAPTER 3

Adapting to the Culture

"Enjoying success requires the ability to adapt. Only by being open to change will you have a true opportunity to get the most from your talent." – Nolan Ryan

As an African-American Project Manager, when you manage projects in the IT or Business world the culture difference becomes glaringly obvious. Transitioning into Project Management or technology can be a major culture shock if you're coming from environments with a good number of minorities. Don't expect to see many other African-Americans meeting you in the break room, walking the halls, and definitely not in the conference room for tactical meetings. The one key thing that you must take away from this section is that there is an unwritten "code" you must understand as an African-American working in a project management and technology environment. Within that code minorities have to be fully aware of more than just their job. In addition to the job you're fighting race-driven perceptions, fitting in, and keeping your identify as an African-American while still being professional.

Project Managers are the face of the project, communicating with technology partners (developers, quality assurance, business analyst) and business partners within the organization. Throughout my career, it's been normal for me to be the only African-American voice on virtual calls and in the conference room for meetings. For myself and many other African-American Project Managers, this issue comes with a lot of stress, uncertainty, and takes a while to get used to. In my early years I wore this as a badge of honor to be the "chose one" that broke through. As I progressed through my career that thought quickly changed from the badge of honor to the one that helped a group with their quota of minorities.

During my years as a Project Manager in most cases I have been the only one or in very few cases I've been one of maybe two or three. They held very entry level roles and in several cases, they held administrative roles to my white Program Manager. Speaking of manager, similar to the lack of upper management representation for minorities, through my years I have never had a black manager that I reported to. As African-Americans in corporate America, we are more accustomed to seeing minorities in the cubicles than in offices behind a desk. That's the reality.

Things to Look Out For

It's important that you be extremely aware and "woke" throughout your tenure as an African-American in a Project Management environment. Observe the words that are used to describe you. Are people constantly complimenting you on how well you speak? I can't count on two hands how many times I've been complimented for how well I speak as if they are surprised that a person of color speaks well. This is a classic example of unintentional racism, where our fellow white colleagues are not aware that their intention to compliment us is actually offensive.

Most blacks that I worked with in a Project Management environment were stakeholders, in most cases these are people that spent many years working on the front-line as call center reps or other type jobs. Working on the project side of the house it's quite normal to work with a white Program Manager, Developer, Quality Assurance Analyst, Business Analyst, and you're the only Project Manager.

Although I've never encountered any blatant racial occurrences, working in a white-dominated environment over a course of fourteen plus years comes with some emotional and mental impacts. At different points in my career, I battled lack of confidence, high levels of stress, and lack of trust in those that I've worked with. I remember on a couple of occasions seeing other Project Managers walking in getting interviews and it felt like the scene in the movie Get Out when Chris first bumped into Andrew. Didn't matter who it was, I was just excited to see another fellow African-American to work with.

Over the years I have connected with many other African-American Project Managers to understand their experiences. It's difficult to hear that many black Project Managers are losing sleep at night because they don't dread the job itself, they dread the environment they are going into. Constantly having to watch your back, watch what you say, how you react, how you walk, how you dress, and will you fit in. These are all stressful things on top of a stressful job.

Lack of Confidence

It's a natural feeling for African-Americans to work in a white-dominated corporate America to suffer occurrences with lack of confidence. Depended upon your mental state, you may be faced with the little voice in your head always wondering if you deserve to be here in this environment. I remember early on in my Project Management career that every mistake or the feeling of messing up on a presentation felt magnified. I literally felt that I was one foot out the door. I struggled with the other little voice of "am I walking or talking too black?" or I would refrain from participating in certain group stories, not the reveal my "black" life. It became overwhelmingly stressful and I completely lost my identity and who I was at the time.

There are many career-killing things that I would often do to sort of bootstrap my lack of confidence just to make it through each day. I would stay away from speaking engagements to prevent myself from being heard by upper management. When I would have one-on-one meetings with my manager the thought of sharing this feeling was in the back of my mind each time. But I refrained from doing so to prevent from getting labeled as the black guy that focused on race.

The reality is if you're faced with lack of confidence on a daily basis you are already one step behind white workers who don't face this issue. As much as you try to hide it, lack of confidence will eventually become evident to others and will be seen that you can't perform when there is a totally different root cause for the lack of confidence white workers can't relate to.

During my mid-year and end of year performance reviews it was common for my feedback to be that I need to take more command of the room. Or I was seen as much laid back and didn't seem to have command of the projects that I worked on. The reality in, I am very laid back but within that I'm aware that I have to watch what I say and be very conscious with how I react. To my surprise during my research with my fellow African-American Project Managers both men and women this was very common feedback.

As an attempt to fix this issue, one gentlemen I spoke with said he intentionally made his voice more forceful in the room. He made a point not to be confrontational, but to have more of a commanding voice on meetings with his project. When his end of year review rolled around the scaled tilted in the opposite direction from being too laid back to basically being called the "mad black man" on the team. His peers felt he came off too aggressive or that he seems like he is always frustrated with his job. As African-Americans in these environments, how do we find our balance? What gives?

Stress

The project management job itself in many cases can be extremely stressful. The project management job as an African-American is even more stressful beyond the scope of the job alone. Instead of just keeping the project on time, within budget, and ensuring that you're building strong relationships. As African-Americans our stress builds beyond those task.

To be a black professional is often to be alone and left on an island. Beyond outright discrimination, which many still face, there are psychological costs to being one of just a few black faces in a predominantly white environment. "In a study of black professional workers in a number of different occupations, it was found that these employees worked to carefully manage their emotions in ways that reflected the racial landscapes they inhabited." Many times I often felt anger, frustration, and annoyed because I felt I had to mask who I am as a person of color.

After I progressed through my career I started to realize that being a person of color working in a Project Management setting was bigger than just myself. I felt the pressure and stress because I felt that my actions or performance would dictate the hiring of other African-Americans. In an upcoming chapter, we will take a deep dive into the aspect of performing for your follow African-Americans to land Project Management roles.

There were many days I wanted to just pack up and quit because I wanted to search for environments where people looked like me and I could relate to. But having a family, paying off debt, wanted to sustain my current lifestyle, I didn't have the luxury of hitting the reset button. So like many of my fellow African-Americans, I had no other choice but to suck it up and "fight the good fight".

When it comes to diversity training in corporations it focuses squarely on hiring practices and treating others fairly across the board. There aren't programs in place to deal with the racial imbalance that's currently occurring across the United States in corporate America. What's scary about diversity programs is that "one study conducted in 2016 stated that of 830 mandatory diversity training programs found that they often triggered a strong backlash against the ideas being promoted." Trainers are reported as stating people often respond to compulsory courses with anger and resistance. With many other participants actually reporting more animosity toward other groups afterwards.

Regardless of the reasons for the glaring ethnic gap in the Project Management environment, it's important to understand what you are signing up for. You must be prepared for being the "only one" in most cases. Be ready to cope and deal with those emotions as they start to creep into your mind. Remember it's not just about you, it's about the other African-American Project Managers trying to break in that you hold a major responsibility for your actions and performance.

This hit me like a ton of bricks one day when we were having a team Lessons Learned meeting using the virtual meeting monitor. We have team members locally in the room with me and in other states across the country. I started to look around and noticed that I was leading a meeting as an African-American man with well over seventy plus team members and I was the only black anywhere in sight. I felt a sense of pride being that I was leading the meeting, but I also felt an urge of sadness and frustration because I know we're not being represented as we should.

Make no mistake about it, adapting to this type of environment can be very difficult and stressful at times. It takes a great bit of mental toughness to work virtually 2080 hours in a year, spending most of your time in a white-dominated environment. Who do you talk to in tough times? Who can you trust and confide in? Who can relate to you and your background? These are all natural questions that come to your mind as an African-American Project Manager. This is all a part of "playing the game".

Over time I learned how to prepare myself for different groups that I'm entering into and how to adapt while I'm there after I'm hired. As you're going through the interview process (given the opportunity) it's important to observe the diversity that currently exists in the group you're interviewing for. There's nothing you can do about the lack of diversity but being observant allows you to make the decision if you're willing to work in that environment and not be surprised.

Being aware of these differences doesn't mean you should react to every situation, as that's just not realistic. But there are cases in which you should make HR aware or at the very least you should have a direct conversation for a common understanding. For instance, I once had a Program Manager who was a white female who flew in to be with our team. It's her first time meeting me, she walks over and told me (not ask) to hold her purse like it was a remake of Driving Miss Daisy, while my white colleagues laughed. This a clear example that she didn't realize how offensive the situation is.

Being aware will allow you to keep your stress in check and boost your confidence as the minority in the group. Remember it's not just you that's facing this issue as this is a nation-wide issue that we have to work together to push through. In the next chapter, we will discuss why it's critical the react appropriately and understand that you hold a greater responsibility to improve the perception of your fellow African-American Project Managers.

CHAPTER 4

Skills Beyond Project Management

"Technical skills may get you the job, but soft skills can make you or break you as a Project Manager"

My mom and dad use to always teach me that you have to be two times better as well as go above and beyond the call of duty. For decades black parents in the U.S. are teaching their children that in order to succeed despite racial discrimination, they need to be "twice as good": twice as smart, twice as dependable, and twice as talented." This translated well for me throughout my Project Management career. I didn't just rely on what was taught to me like the traditional Project Manager. I remained curious and proactively seeking out ways to improve my skills giving me the best chance to stick out amongst my competition but particularly white that dominated the environment. Parents of white workers and specifically white Project Managers do not have to deal with the extra layer to teaching the two times better lesson.

It's simply not enough to be an African-American Project Manager that's just viewed as "good". Research shows that you must be a great communicator, great with managing risks, providing strategic value. Certifications are important which is why I obtained my Scrum Masters certification, PMP, and MBA in Project Management. I would purposely insert myself into being the owner of certain processes and systems so that I could be the thought leader and a necessity to my team.

Research supports why the "two times" better teaching by black parents is a crucial step not only in life but in the corporate world as well. It's critical to fill your knowledge toolbox with as many project methodologies as possible, technical skills, learn vital topics to your organization, and just about any personal development that's made available to you. The perception of the African-American worker is low and lacks the confidence of our fellow white colleagues and upper management. Out of one-hundred African-American Project Managers that I interviewed, eighty percent felt they were held back because of their blackness, not because of their lack of skills.

It's important to not lose sight and just identify yourself as a Project Manager. In reality, you are an African-American Project Manager, and you are definitely viewed as such throughout the organization. You are the classic example of the elephant in the room in a white-dominated environment. But it's important that you fight through this with your skills and not your attitude (as expected) or most importantly your mouth.

Be aware that being exceptional at our job as an African-American does come with a cost. Research supports that blacks that appear confident and knowledgeable at their jobs are perceived as arrogant and over-confident. But that should not deter you from building of your knowledge base and excelling as an African-American Project Manager. In order to give you a full understanding of how to build your skills beyond the basic Project Management fundamentals, I'm going to break down the areas that can separate you from the competition:

SharePoint

Microsoft SharePoint is an awesome collaborative tool that can be leveraged to provide a more coordinated environment to track and manage a project with your team and stakeholders. At the basic level, you can create documents and upload them for others on your project team to review and/or edit. Pretty much any user can easily pick up the basic functionalities of using SharePoint. Project Managers are normally the owners of these sites to structure their project and make documents easy to find for the team.

It's the advanced skills in SharePoint that will separate you as a Project Manager. You can create basic and stylish pages, set up workflows to approve documents, or even set up a Gantt Chart to track your timeline. The advanced skills have allowed me to stick out a Project Manager amongst my competition. In my experience most Project Managers I've worked with focuses on the basic fundamentals of Project Management. They don't take the time to learn these skills, but more and more managers are expecting that you have this skill set in your toolbox.

There is not an excuse why you cannot easily enhance your skills in SharePoint because organizations provide on the job training both in class and on-demand learning. If for some reason that's not made available to you, there are websites like www.udacity.com and www.udemy.com that are very inexpensive to teach you these skills.

Microsoft Excel

Microsoft Excel has largely been used to input data and create reports. But in the Project Management world, Excel has become a staple to not only manage the project timeline, but to manage issues, risks, create change request forms, and other forms of tracking throughout the project.

Although there are many project shops that endorse solely using Microsoft Project, many others still would prefer to use Excel because it's flexibility for all users throughout the project team. MS Project a user must have a license, which could be pretty expensive to provide for every user on the project, and even great if you include all other stakeholders.

Excel has the capabilities to perform parallel functions as MS Project but it does come with a learning curve. At the advanced level, you must be able to appropriately format columns, rows, and cells in order to create your platform from scratch. Creating formulas is a critical advanced skill because it allows you to automate calculations of time just but entering in data in certain fields. This makes using MS Excel a very powerful tool to manage projects and intuitive for all users within the project.

Another power skill is using Pivot Tables which allows you to take the data on one page and create custom reports. In cases where upper management wants to analyze what the data means that's currently living in your Excel spreadsheet, you can easily provide that to them.

Being able to perform at an advanced level as a Project Manager is a sure way to separate yourself from your fellow Project Managers. As an African-American

Project Manager, it puts you in a high demand pool of talent for recruiters and organizations as a whole.

Development Languages

When it comes to learning development languages like HTML, Java, Python, and others. I'm not at all saying that you must go out and get a Computer Science degree. But considering that you will be working in project environments that are technical in nature, it helps to understand what developers are doing. This also makes being able to understand various status updates developers are providing you than communicating back to the business partners on your team in a manner they can understand.

Being able to understand the technical aspects of a project opens up more opportunities in your project career. Throughout my career, I've worked as both a Business and Technical Project Manager, and it's the understanding the various development languages that enhanced my abilities. You can go to just about any local community college or the previous sites that I mentioned above, Udacity or Udemy to learn.

As a Technical Project Manager this will enhance your ability to understand the work developers are doing on your team. You will be able to communicate status updates back to your business partners in more of a confident way.

PowerPoint

Microsoft PowerPoint is a staple when it comes to managing projects mostly used for demos and reporting on various aspects of your project. Just as with the previous tools, there are both basic and advanced skills that can be utilized to separate the skill-set of various Project Managers. At the basic level, PowerPoint is pretty easy to pick up. You are able to use drag and drop functionality to create slides with text, shapes, images, graphs, other reporting capabilities.

As a Project Manager, in some cases, you are required to create executive level reports which are highly visible throughout upper management. You have to be to creatively take large amounts of data from various reports and display it on one slide so that it's easily digestible for executives to understand. This requires the ability to combine various shapes, text, colors, and graphs and display professionally.

Being able to master this skillset is another key way to not only land Project Management opportunities but to impress executives on your level of presentation skills. Not everyone is born with the creative gene like an artist, but enhancing your PowerPoint skills will allow you to become more creative over time.

In summary, it's important that you think beyond the fundamental aspects of being a Project Manager, especially as an African-American. As opposed to complaining about lack of job opportunities for minorities and posting on social media, strengthening your skills how you truly counter-attack this nation-wide issue. Reports show that "there is a huge wealth and income disparity between blacks and whites in American (average wealth of white families was more than $500,000 higher than African-Americans in 2013 and whites in 2015 earned $25.22 an hour, on average, compared with $18.49 for blacks." Racial inequality as a whole we can't completely erase due to most of the hiring decision-makers are white. But enhancing your skills as an African-American can make it very difficult for your skill-set to be overlooked for promotions and landing new opportunities. Bottom line, it's up to you to put the control in your hands.

In the next chapter, you will learn why it's important to consistently network and build relationships with mentors as an African-American Project Manager. Landing a Project Management job is half the battle, but growing and advancing your career will require help from other experienced people. Many may not think so, but networking is a skill as well, but in the next chapter you will learn the skills to navigate the waters of networking.

CHAPTER 5

Networking & Mentors

"Emerging leaders need mentors to guide them, but they also need a network of peers to reassure them that they are not on the path alone." – Alyse Nelson

You've heard the saying many times over, "it's not what you know but who you know that truly matters" when it comes to excelling in your career. Especially in project management. Throughout my career, I have been blessed to have great mentors who are willing to guide me and provide meaningful opportunities for growth. My mentors not only taught me about what is important (both personally and professionally) but they have also given me several big breaks along the way. Don't think having a mentor is important? Here are the numbers to support why you're wrong... "Based on Glassdoor's numbers, your chances of getting an acceptable offer are a "statistically significant" 2.6% to 6.6% higher if you were referred by a current employee than if you weren't." The numbers may seem small in nature but this confirms what we all should recognize and know that connections matter, and yes, you should develop the networking mindset quickly. "Boosting the odds of getting a job offer by roughly 5% would mean on average that one in twenty workers get a job offer who wouldn't have otherwise gotten one." This is especially critical for African-Americans in the workplace where there is a significant gap in hiring.

While having mentors is great, but as an African-American professional, it's critical that you seek out other experienced African-American professionals as well. This has been critical for me throughout my Project Management career. Finding other experienced Project Managers can be difficult as we know we don't dominate this space especially at the management level. It's not a difficult task and professional social sites like LinkedIn has made it much easier to network with my mobile devices or laptops. Additionally, Meetup groups and company provided diversity programs makes it easier for users to network and find mentors of color. If you haven't started networking and now starting to understand the importance... you may be asking yourself, "how do I get started?" Below I'm going to share some tips on how to start networking and build your circle of mentors and especially those of color.

How to Start Networking

In many cases, networking may feel a lot like sales which most of us, especially Project Managers aren't very good at and no desire to sell anything. It's much different than striking up a normal conversation about good food, the game that was on last night or a good movie. The reason it feels that way is because we know in the back of our minds we are reaching out to a person with the intent of something we need. That usually comes with an answer of "yes" or "no" and as human beings, we hate hearing the word no. So naturally, we try our best to avoid situations where we could likely hear "no" because it's painful. But to break the bad news to you, when you're networking just like in sales you will often hear no a lot. Even worse as an

African-American, not only will you hear the word "no" but it will be difficult to find potential candidates to network within line with your future goals.

Mindset

Networking all starts with developing the right mindset. Your goal isn't to solely just see how many people you can get to help you advance your career. Your primary goal is to focus or develop the mindset of building relationships. Without first developing this mindset it doesn't matter how many people you beg to help you or send messages to their inbox, it simply will not happen. People will smell a selfish attitude a mile away and will emphatically send a no your way or even worse ignore you. This is the biggest mistake I made over the course of my years connecting with people is not focusing on relationships first. I was too much in a rush caring about my own career and the outcome of what I could get out of people. A relationship happens over a course of a few conversations, once you've established a connection then you can introduce your needs but always offer help from your end as well.

Don't just call people up when you need something, instead proactively call and get in the habit of routine check-ins. It's during those check-ins that you're building and nurturing the relationship. They may be in need of assistance and you may be in position to help them along the way. This is the way you build up what I call relationship equity with people. Without having your relationship equity built up, it can be difficult to make they call for help (or withdrawal) when you desperately need it most.

Network Events

No matter what city you live in, there are networking events happening today, this week, or even the following week. Networking does not mean you have to network with people exactly in your same profession as a Project Manager. Although ideal, but don't restrict yourself to only looking for Project Management networking groups. Instead look for professional groups that will have a balance of gender and ethnic backgrounds. Keeping in mind the goal of building relationships, don't try to attend events one time and try to get mentorship connections all in one swoop. Instead, make a habit of attending and getting recognized as a consistent member. Volunteer to play key roles where you see fit to provide a contribution. This will allow you to quickly get recognized. Observe who the key contributors are in the group and make sure you introduce yourself to them. This will accelerate key introductions for you throughout the various groups. I get it, after work we're busy with other activities with family or other things. But if you want to excel as an African-American professional in general especially a Project Manager, you must master networking.

Networking events do not just occur outside of your working environments, but they also occur on many occasions inside your working environments. Working at a Fortune 500, we have access to different groups for all races (Project Management Body of Knowledge) and groups specifically for minorities and other niche or ethnic groups. These are effective ways to network because they consist of people already working at the same organization (immediate ice-breaker) and a great opportunity to meet people in key positions to advance your career.

One of the key strategies I used is to network within my company is to look at the job board every day. This gave me the ability to know which groups are hiring, the managers name, and I would reach out to their direct reports and offer to buy them coffee to learn about their group. Always had a key contact within the group and had direct insight into how the environment is. How the much the group is growing? How much re-organization is going on? Are there any lay-offs happening? How diverse the group is? I kept a little black book of contacts and notes for each group.

LinkedIn

Innovative solutions like LinkedIn has open up opportunities for many professionals to network 24/7 right from your mobile device or laptop. There is strength in numbers and LinkedIn has the numbers that work in your favor. "LinkedIn has millions of members in more than two-hundred countries, including executives from all Fortune 500 companies." Individuals use LinkedIn for professional networking, connecting, and job searching. Conversely, companies use LinkedIn for recruiting and for providing company information to prospective employees. So it's obvious your LinkedIn profile should look nothing like your Facebook profile…. Simply put, keep it professional!

LinkedIn allows you not only see the pictures but the full profiles and work history of millions of professionals around the world. You can search for people by the professional, company, and location. You're also given the opportunity to connect with them and to send the private messages to initiate the conversation and potentially take your relationship building journey offline (phone call and/or Skype).

LinkedIn continues to be critical to the advancement of my career and to build my network of mentors across the world. When I'm not attending local networking events, I'm constantly reaching out connect with other like-minded professionals. Just like with traditional face-to-face networking, networking online comes with some unwritten rules and etiquette. Below are some common best practices that you must follow for online networking success:

1. Have the mindset of building relationships first.

2. Read their profile, understand where they live, what they do, where they have and currently work.

3. Introduce yourself with a personalized message and get straight to the point with why you're reaching out to them.

4. Don't send along one or two paragraph message; keep it brief and straight to the point

5. End with offering to help them in any way you can by your personal skills or introductions

A sample message that I generally use:

Hello [name] –

I reviewed your profile and really impressed with the work you've done for XYZ Company. My career path closely lines up with what you're doing. I would like to get 10-15 minutes of your time to further learn what you do and offer any help that I can as well.

Please let me know if you have any availability this week

Kind regards,

Eric Pannell

As you can see I keep if brief, personalized to the person I'm reaching out to and straight to the point with my intentions. This has been an effective strategy for me which has allowed me to build a network of mentors that I can call on of well over two-hundred plus people.

LinkedIn is a great way to become more knowledgeable about different companies and to fast-track connecting with people within the current company you work at. With the right mindset and focus you can develop a solid network around the world pretty quickly. Just like anything, it takes time, but focus and consistency is the key.

Shapr

As of recent, there is another app that I like to use called Shapr which is a Tinder-like app for professionals to network using your mobile phone. You can connect with professionals using the swipe mobile, giving you a faster way to connect with other like-minded professionals. Using the same strategy that you just learned from LinkedIn applies to using Shapr. This app is available for both iPhone and Android.

Networking While Black

It's important to understand that while networking is critical, but networking while black there are a whole different set of rules. Networking is the right thing to do but you also must understand that people are more prone to help others that look like them. A study done in 2013 supports this by the Public Religion Research Institute which revealed that "about seventy-five percent of white Americans don't have any non-white friends. About sixty-five percent of black

Americans don't have any white friends, according to the study." These numbers are alarming and it doesn't say that black and whites don't fully like each other rather it speaks volumes that we associate more with who look, talk, and act like us. Americans, white and black, live virtually segregated lives, and since advantages, privileges and economic progress have already accrued in favor of whites, the additional advantages that flow from this help go almost exclusively to whites.

This is why it's important for you to cross the barrier of getting comfortable with networking with white professionals but specifically experience black professionals. You get the experience of digging down a deeper layer to discuss key topics beyond the on the job requirements. You can learn about the "black experience" in various working environments. The number of blacks in the Project Management Office (PMO), on the development team, in upper management, etc. These are important aspects that you must learn from your experience as an African-American Project Manager. Most importantly you're more likely to "be yourself" when speaking with another fellow African-American.

Recruiting young African-American professionals has become a top priority for many large companies. While hiring African-American talent is improving, the major issue lays with keeping them in-house and getting them to stay. Retention is one of the key issues as many African-Americans struggle navigating the workplace. Large corporations are doing a poor job of identifying and developing their black talent pool. One research interview concluded that "Successful African-American executives indicated that relationship building was more complex for them and required special effort to connect with their minority culture peers. This was particularly evident when discussing activities outside of work hours such as business dinners with colleagues, attending corporate events, and the like. Many African-

American executives eschew these events, preferring to spend these off hours at home with their families or other close connections where they can take off their mask and recharge for the next day."

It's important that you understand that networking and networking while black lives in their own separate universe. When networking with white professionals it's about building your "who you know" connections, networking while black is about diving in a deeper level to understand the survival guide as an African-American in a white-dominated corporate world.

You've heard the phrase "taking off your mask" when it comes to describing the black professional in corporate America. One of the key things you will learn when connecting with working African-American professions is the ability to be yourself (professionally). It's OK to be yourself, be black, and to be viewed as professional in a corporate setting. You can fake not being yourself in the short-term but there are many identity and mental health issues that will catch up to you in the long-run.

Networking is vital to growth and development of your project management career, especially as an African-American. Remember the phrase A.B.N…. Always Be Networking! You must be consistent and intentional with your networking strategy. Although you will never see it emphasize in your project management studies, it is however a critical part of your "personal" job to ensure that you do it. A question I want you to ask yourself today… who is that person that you can call on when you lose your job that can help you quickly get back on track? If your answer is "I don't know" then it's time to work on your networking strategy.

CHAPTER 6

Be Black (Professionally)

"Don't change so people will like you. Be yourself and the right people will love the real you."

There are generally two types of black people in the office which comes with both their positives and negatives: one is the person at work who offers insight into the "black experience" or the person in the office whose only mission is to show up at work and not be seen as black. I have many times been faced with this issue during my many years in corporate America. Deciding how to disclose what movies I watch, sitcoms I regularly watch, music I listen to, and even the type of food I eat. Because all of those situations come with such race sensitivity, it's easy as a black person to hide those things which makes up who you are. The key question: Does your work identity match your personal identity? If you're like most, probably not.

When I landed my first project management job I honestly didn't even notice that I was one of few African-Americans in the office. I was so excited that I reached my goal at the time I was just focused on holding on, learning and excelling. It wasn't until I started facing challenges that I realized that I didn't have anyone I was comfortable with to turn to. I didn't want to be seen as the "black guy" complaining and having problems adapting to the environment. I started seeing hire after hire be people that don't look like me and I quickly started to realize that it's either a coincidence or black people just do not want to work in project management. I was honestly confused.

To make matters worse, one day my manager (who is white) we met up for lunch, and we started talking about our projects and work overall. He said to me that he was tired of working for "the man". With a look of confusion on my face, I'm sure he could tell I was completely confused. In my head, "you have no idea". We still talk to this day and I'm not sure if he has ever figured out that he represents "the man". But in all reality, he is a great guy and we still talk to this day.

There are however many stereotypical issues that cloud the mental state of the black professional in the office. Things like… what do I wear? Should I say this or say that? Should I admit that I listen to this or listen to that? Should I admit that I like eating chicken or drinking flavored sodas? While writing this book I reached out to many African-American Project Managers for them to share their experiences.

During my research conducted with various Black Project Managers by asking the following question: "Please share what you do or don't do to not appear 'too Black" in your office:

- I tend to agree with my fellow white co-workers to be more a part of the group and not showing my "black" preference.

- I keep my anger or frustrations in check to not be perceived as the "angry black man."

- I will purposely change my voice to my audience when I hold meetings to appear more intelligent with the words that I use.

- I don't admit that I listen to rap music in most cases or will avoid the question altogether.

- I keep my facial expressions in check to not appear offended by certain topics or comments being discussed.

- I will jump at the thought of any disappointment expressed by my boss even when I'm working my hardest.

These comments are a reality that black professionals live across the country in corporate America. It's important that you become aware of them and recognize you're guilty of them and now is the time to correct them and be who you are professionally.

When you take a step back and realize that as a Project Manager, in general, it comes with several exceptional skills regardless what color you are. Skills such as relationship building, listening, communication, team building, leadership, and many others. The mere fact that you're managing a project of any size as an African-American speaks volumes to your abilities. Regardless if you may be the "token" black in the office, once you're in the seat it's up to you to put your skills on display, be professional, and most important embrace being black by being you. So that begs the question… how do you going about "being you?".

Over the years I've put into practice several strategies that allows me to not only display my worth to my fellow white colleagues but to most importantly sleep well at night knowing that I'm being myself.

Find Your Voice

In the black community, we have a code in which how we speak or address one another with a handshake. You've likely seen it on display when former President Barak Obama was on the way out of the White House and he greets the janitor on the way out the door. There's a certain gesture that black men greet one another in passing in the grocery store with a slight head nod up that follows with a "what's up". Conversely, when I'm in the office or passing a white person that gesture now becomes a head nod in the opposite direction with a verbal following of, "hello, how are you doing".

The point I'm making is we speak differently around people we know and feel comfortable within the office than outside the office. Especially when you're black. But within that, it's important to be professional and embrace who you are. Normally outside of work I have a heavier tone, more forcefulness in my voice, maybe even talked slower. The reason I did that was to hedge off any perception that I was too aggressive or appear to sound too black. Don't make this mistake as it will backfire on you in the long-run. Don't be ashamed to practice this over time, find your professional voice, one that will allow you to feel comfortable regardless. who you talk to in the office.

Be Consistent

Many times we talk one way to one of our colleagues and a totally different way when it comes to talking to another. But what happens when you're in the presence of both of them at the same time. Which person are you going to be now? This is a key reason why you must be consistent and stick to who you truly are 100% of the time. Besides, it very difficult and way too much work to be pretending to be someone you're not.

I've found that it's critical to own who you are as a Black Project Manager, regardless of the current circumstances that come with working in a white-dominated environment. Not doing some comes with a price to your mental and emotional state. People (white and black) will respect you more if you're consistent and be who you are all the time. They will look more at what you deliver in terms of your skills as opposed to your blackness.

Do Not Participate in Every Conversation

You may be one of those people that like to socialize in every conversation, which is fine. But there are some conversations that it's OK to stay away from. When it comes to political conversations, such as the "Trump-era" that we're in now. Don't be so quick to hop in and voice your opinion. There are many sitcoms and movies that present a racial connotation to them. In some cases, your follow white colleagues may not find any issues with laughing at those jokes right in front of your face. If it gets too out of hand there are protocols in place to speak with your manager or even speaking with HR.

But the reality is we choose what we should and shouldn't be offended by. I've made a career out taking the high road and focusing on the things that matter to me most which is excelling in my career and taking care of my family. Ask anyone of my white colleagues they will tell you that I'm easily approachable, laid back, and the complete team player. But I've evolved to giving myself permission to be not only a professional Project Manager but a professional "black" Project Manager by being me.

There are popular events that has occurred that has divided us culturally, meaning black and white. Two popular instances are Michael Vick with his dog fighting case, and of course O.J. This is popular water cooler chatter that will occur in break rooms in corporate America across the country. Keys to remember… where you are and who you are? It's a losing battle that you don't want to fight and most importantly this is a great opportunity to put you on the bad list to lose your job.

Earn Respect

Earning respect in a white-dominated project environment means being professional in every aspect and setting the tone for who you truly are. You, unfortunately, don't get many chances to make this impression. This includes how you talk, how you dress, and how you treat others. This of course doesn't mean you have to sell your soul, not saying that at all. But this is a great opportunity to show what you can do.

Don't shy away from the tasks or opportunities that comes up outside of your general job description. Get comfortable with volunteering tough tasks like setting up a new process for your group. Putting together a process flow to highlight bottlenecks or key pain point areas in the way your group or organization carries out your daily operation.

This opportunity is a game-changer to put on display truly how talented you are. Remember doing this is not all about you because there is a perception with African-American Project Managers that we're just happy or lucky to be here. You should be proud to stand up to show not only what you can personally do but also show that African-American Project Managers can excel at this role.

You're not only letting yourself down by remaining quiet and just merely getting by or doing "enough" to earn a paycheck. But your current and aspiring Project Managers need you to take a stand and help change the perception to open up doors. Doing so will allow you to earn not only respect but overtime you will become a valued commodity within your group.

Lose the Attitude

Remember the vibe you sent through your interview process as being professional and the ultimate team member? Earning the perception of being too aggressive or having an attitude can crumble that with one or too many occurrences. This is especially true for women of color in corporate America. A study was done by the Center for Women Policy Studies "found twenty-one percent of women of color surveyed did not feel they were free to be themselves at work. The same study found more than one-third of women of color—ranging from twenty-eight percent to forty-four percent—believed that they must "play down" their race or ethnicity to succeed." Be firm but don't lose your cool and focus on winning an argument or being right at work. Place more emphasis on doing the right thing.

Many times as African-Americans in corporate America we let the "system" get the best of us and visibly get frustrated. This not only hurts you but it sets a bad example for many other African-Americans fighting the corporate fight along with you. It is critical that we keep our emotions and attitudes in check, and focus on being professional as the top priority.

In the next chapter, we're going to talk about knowing who your enemies and advocates are. Unfortunately, you really can't control either of those but what you can control is how you identify them and foster the relationships with your advocates. Research shows that many working African-Americans struggle because they lack key influencer sponsors or advocates.

Probably the greatest and most motivational book I've read of all time is Black Privilege by Charlamagne Tha God. His very first chapter opens up with "It's Not the Size of the Pond but the Hustle in the Fish" In which I think all African-Americans can draw from while working in Corporate America. He starts this chapter with a quote that speaks to me and how we should temper our attitudes:

"Geographical location doesn't determine what kind of success you will have, but your psychological position always well. How are you going to make waves in a bigger pond when you haven't even learned how to cause a ripple in the pond you're in? When you stop complaining about where you are physically and start focusing on where you are mentally, that's when you will start to transcend your circumstances."

This is a phenomenal book, and I highly recommend that anyone but especially African-Americans read this book.

CHAPTER 7

Know Your Enemies & Advocates

"The best leaders not only develop us, they advocate our future" – Michael Dooley

Knowing who your enemies and sponsors (or advocates) are is extremely critical to the progression of your career. This is especially true as an African-American professional in the workplace. The good ole boy network that was once rampant throughout corporate America still exist although not as obvious. The types of sponsorships to accelerate careers that exist for white males through the shared interest in sports, familiarity, fraternities and sororities aren't as easily accessible for African-Americans.

It would be unfair for me to not mention the corporates version of "black-on-black" crime that takes place within the workplace. Because of the stress and the difficulties of "making it" as an African-American in the corporate world adds some extra tension amongst ourselves. Be on the lookout for other African-American who want nothing more than to see you fail for their gain of potential promotion or perception in the eyes of those in power (mostly whites). Sad to admit but I have personally been faced with this issue many times throughout my career.

Mentoring is a great avenue to enhance the careers of African-Americans, but that alone will not solve the issues of inequality in the workplace. While mentoring shouldn't be entirely discounted, its widespread adoption hasn't helped women and minorities penetrate the executive ranks like sponsorship programs can. Women occupy only four percent of the CEO seats at Fortune 500 companies, and nine-teen percent of its board seats, according to the Catalyst Research. And there are only five African-American CEOs in the Fortune 500. People and programs speaking on the behalf of African-American professionals is the key to increase the share of workers and creating stability with keeping black workers in their positions.

Seventy percent of men and sixty-eight percent of women with sponsors felt more satisfied with their career advancement, compared to fifty-seven percent of both men and women without sponsors. Even more encouraging is that minority employees with sponsors were sixty-five percent more satisfied than non-sponsored employees.

Outside of sponsorship programs, similar to mentors, it's critical that you identify and connect with those who are willing to sponsor you. These are people, regardless of color, that are in positions to either directly hire you or have the influence to speak with others to hire you. Most sponsors will come inside your direct group in which you currently work. The sponsor/worker relationship is built over time by fostering strong relationships and producing "A" level work. It's not fair to think that someone should speak up on your behalf if you're don't producing quality work, and risk putting their reputation on the line.

I've made my project management career out of identifying and building strong relationships with sponsors. There is nothing more powerful than when it's time to apply for a job you can have a quick conversation and jump to the front of the line because someone else believes in you. This is very true for African-Americans that are faced with hiring issues because their name is too black on their resume, or they are passed over because another white Project Manager made the right connections. A study conducted with several recruiters reported that, "after responding to 1,300 ads with more than 5,000 resumes, the researchers found that the job applicants with white names needed to send ten resumes to get one callback, but the black candidate needed to send fifteen for one" Which further supports the need of having an advocate by going through the back door to get ideal jobs.

How Do I Connect With Advocates in a Project Environment?

There are three key people and roles that you must ensure are on your side as a Project Manager. The Program Manager which is generally the person who manages the Project Managers, the Business Sponsor which is the person who represents the business in which initiated the project and has the highest interest. If you're working on a technical project, you need to make sure you have the Lead Developer on your side. As I mentioned earlier in the book I have never had a black Program Manager or lead developer and throughout my fourteen plus years as a Project Manager, I've only worked with one black sponsor who managed a group of mortgage loan processors who were largely black. Sounds strategic or coincidence?

Aside from your voice as the Project Manager, these are generally the loudest voices that will be heard or will make key decisions throughout the project. They each hold their own importance that I will break down.

Sponsor

The project sponsor is an individual (often a manager or executive) with overall accountability for the project. He or she is primarily concerned with ensuring that the project delivers the agreed upon business benefits and acts as the representative of the organization, playing a vital leadership role through a series of areas:

- Provides the necessary expertise and context; appoints resources

- Selling the benefits of the project throughout the organization

- Serves as an escalation point for decisions for issues and risks

- Acts as a connection point between the project and the business community

All of this to say in short that the Project Sponsor carries a lot of weight not only for the success of your project but additionally the longevity of your existence working on their projects. Being that in most cases Project Sponsors are predominantly white, it's critical as a black Project Manager that you go above and beyond to nurture that relationship.

Your Program Manager will generally have on-going meetings with your Sponsor and their colleagues. One of the key conversations that always surfaces is the productivity of the fleet of Project Managers that are working on their projects. The conversation that you're shooting for is for project sponsors to proactively make requests for you to work on their projects. This displays that you have built the right relationships, the sponsor and likely their direct reports like you, and you will have proven that you are an effective Project Manager. But in order to get there, it takes more than just being a "good" Project Manager to get there.

Many black Project Managers that I've worked with allow them being the one or few Project Managers to just come in and just focus on project management work then ignore building relationships. Here are some best practices to turn your sponsor into and fan or raving advocate for you:

Set Up Weekly 1-on-1 Meetings:

This is not an optional task unless your project sponsor is too busy to agree with this. But in most cases, they will definitely want this level of communication. This is your 1-on-1 time with your project sponsor to talk about the project overall, issues, risks, potential escalation points, how the team is gelling together, and anything not related to the project. This is a great opportunity to start nurturing the relationship. Start to know the personal likes and dislikes of your sponsor, what the like to do outside of work, any special interests, family life, etc. This is an opportunity for them to get to know you beyond work as well. Which is critical when it comes to building relationships as an African-American and connecting with advocates. The more human you appear as opposed to just another Project Manager (especially black), you are able to eliminate any perceptions that may be lingering in their minds.

It's critical that you understand the importance of building and maintain strong relationships with the project sponsor. Any feeling or mention to your Program Manager about your performance in a negative light it will greatly enhance any negative perceived thoughts about you as a black Project Manager and put a strain on your employment. Not at all saying that you have to sell your soul, but it's important to take the right steps to build the relationship.

If you take the right steps to build a relationship with your sponsor, they will more than likely become advocates for you for future work. They will make a special request to have you work on their projects, recommend you to their peers for their projects. Serve as a strong resource for you when it comes time for promotion.

Lead Developer

When you're working on a technical project you will have to get used to working with technical resources like architects, developers, systems analyst, etc. But it is the Lead Developer that normally carries the weight of the project. Their role could be strictly from a management perspective or more hands-on doing the day-to-day work. Regardless of their role, it is critical that you win them over similar to the project sponsor.

Technical teams are normally stick together pretty tight and what the lead or more experience developer thinks carries a lot of weight. So naturally, if you don't win them over, it's highly unlikely you're going to win the team over. Similar to the project sponsor make sure that you set up some one-on-one time with the lead developer. Talk about communication styles, get to know how the team likes to work with Project Managers, show your human side, and give him or her an opportunity to truly know you.

Having both the project sponsor and the lead developer speaking highly of you is an effective way to accelerate your career. Without building these relationships up, it's highly like you're going to struggle to manage your project constantly dealing with personality issues, etc. Remember as a black Project Manager, you are the face of other black Project Managers who will come behind you. It's critical to put your best foot forward to set the example for others and to change the perception.

Program Manager

The Program Manager normally is the person that hired you and manages your day-to-day work. They normally managing other Project Managers on your team and manage a portfolio of projects including your project. In the eyes of your Program Manager, this is your time to shine and stick out amongst your other fellow Project Managers. It's likely your experience has been like mine in most of my environments, I'm generally the only black. Not only do you have to compete in general as a Project Manager but it's critical that you show that as a black Project Manager you are more than capable of doing the work.

Making a point to establish advocates within the organization is vital to the longevity of your career development. Especially as a black professional and Project Manager it's a sure way to cross the barrier and reap the benefits of our fellow professional works.

In the next chapter, we will discuss why the work that you do as a black professional and Project Manager is bigger than you. It's important that you see the work that you do changes the perception of the black professionals in the workplace. A study shows that there is a bad perception that exists and its evident in the lack of minorities in technology overall and especially as Project Managers.

CHAPTER 8

Breaking The Cycle

"Change is hard at first, messy in the middle and gorgeous at the end." – Robin Sharma

I started to name this chapter Stick to the Tribe, but I thought that would send a negative message and I wouldn't get my point across. So I changed it to Breaking the Cycle because as African-American in corporate America and in this case Project Managers we have a responsibility to break the cycle. With all the stereotypes and perceptions that whites have about African-Americans in the workplace, it's up to you to change that on a daily basis to help us all. You've heard them all:

- We're not knowledgeable or capable to manage large projects
- We talk, dress and act too black in the workplace
- We're too aggressive or confrontational

These are all perceptions that exist which prevents us making our mark in corporate American and creating a more diverse working environment. But once we are blessed to get our foot in the door it's important that you consciously approach every day to change the perception of blacks in corporate America. I made this conscious effort not only by writing this book but through my actions very early in my project management career.

I feel it's my obligation and duty that when an African-American reaches out to me for help or guidance in the Project Management space I create time for that discussion. It's not about getting the job, it's much bigger than that. I have an obligation to help someone support their family better, understand the African-American experience in the workplace and project management environment.

We should join the various diversity groups with the mindset to help one another and further educate each other about the realities of minorities in the workplace. If we are in positions of power, if formal processes aren't in place, we should create them for people of color to have an outlet for career advancement. Take a stand and create local events using tools like Eventbrite or Meetups to bring minority college students or people looking to transition their careers into Project Management.

Making six figures per year seems to be the pinnacle for most people to reach in their careers and that is very doable as a Project Manager. Unfortunately, many African-American Project Managers that I've spoken to feel that they've "made" it once they reached that point. Landing a six-figure project management job doesn't mean you made it at all. It just means that you're now chosen to reach back to help our fellow *"brothas"* and *"sistas"* to great more equality and help corporate America create more diversity.

Every Action Matters

When you first read the title of this book there are many emotions and reactions that can be drawn from it. For blacks working the Project Management industry, I'm sure it draws you in and instantly reminds of you all the experiences (inequality, stereotypes, perceptions, etc.) that you've faced along the way. For whites, it may come off very controversial simply because as history has shown us, discussing race is very difficult. You may even think that only blacks should take the time to read this book but I would argue against that point. I think this book presents an opportunity to raise awareness around the world and allow us (blacks and whites) to work together a make a change.

If there's anything that I want you to take away from this book it's that every little action you individually take matters. The time you take to educate others, looking past your perceptions, being courteous, professionalism, building "real" relationships beyond the work, with the sole focus of looking at people as a human being with exceptional skills and not the color of their skin. I proudly wear the badge as a black Project Manager who is looking to help other aspiring and struggling Project Managers.

As African-Americans regardless how many wrong-doings you've faced with our fellow white colleagues, still find hope that there are white professionals who are more than willing to help you. It's your job to stay persistent and find them. Keep a positive mindset, stick to your tribe of black professionals, but continue to build solid relationships regardless of color.

When you're in environments where you're one of few blacks instead of focusing on that aspect look at it as an opportunity to change the perception of our fellow black professionals. Focus on being the best professional you can be and not the black elephant in the room. Focusing more on those emotions will instantly put you in a negative mindset and will you with more unnecessary stress.

Hard work will always be the key ingredient to allow us to reach our goals and what we truly want out of life, regardless of race. But just like my parents always taught me, you must understand that the rules are different for blacks, we must work two times harder. And that's OK. It just means that you have to increase your knowledge toolbox to make that happen. With all the inexpensive training courses made available to use at the tip of our fingers, it's even easier to do.

Embrace and Own It...

Further, this book is meant to enhance our abilities to embrace being black as professionals and specifically in the project environment. Far too many of us feel scared, lack confidence, and feel completely out of place in less diverse environments. Embrace that you are different, talk different, walk with a swag of confidence, and may talk differently than our white colleagues. It's perfectly OK. The key is that you also embrace a professional posture and put your skills on display daily. People will always have their perceptions, but the one they can never ignore is your skills, how successfully you manage your projects, and the key relationships you build along the way. You must own and wear your badge as a black successful professional in corporate American and what it truly represents. It means that we have another one of "us" in position to help one another.

Change is a must and if you watched the movie 'Remember the Titans' you saw a clash of everything that describes change and inequality in corporate America. When the Titans headed off to training, they were divided, black versus white, new versus old; change versus history. In order for Coach Boone (Denzel Washington) to unify all of his players, coaches included, to create a team that cohesively worked together has had to change the way the team practices on the field and how they lived. In the movie he says,

"Everything we do is change. We gon' change the way we run. We gon' change the way we eat. We gon' change the way we block. We gon' change the way we tackle. We gon' change the way we win."

Throughout my experience as a minority Project Manager, change has been one of the hardest and difficult inevitabilities corporate America has thrown at me. It's a lot like this movie. We're comfortable being around who looks like us, walk like us, or talk like us. The only problem is most people that look like "us" as African-Americans aren't walking the halls with us in tech and project management spaces. The key is to understand that change is necessary for our survival in corporate America. And it's critical to understand that if you can't change your way of thinking and impact the change of others you will have a tough run during your journey as an African-American Project Manager and life in general.

ACKNOWLEDGEMENTS

Writing a book for the first time is hard, but writing this portion of the book is extremely difficult for me. I have so many people to thank for both the good and bad experiences that I fear making people mad for not mentioning them individually. Please understand that if I do not mention you individually, please know that I love you and words can't possibly express how thankful I am for you.

I want to first give glory to God for taking me on this journey that I've been on for the past 39 years of my life. Not sure where I would be without God always in my heart, loving me, guiding me, watching over me 24/7. It all starts there that I can't do anything without God by my side.

Next I want to thank my family, my beautiful wife Tara, my kids, Jadon and Jeremiah. They have seen be walk through the door happy, sad, and angry, but to see their face when I walk through the door makes it all worth it. As we all know that life is not fair, but it makes it all worth it when you have that place of peace and people that love you to lift you up. I truly love you and I appreciate you for always encouraging me and allowing me to pursue my dreams.

To my parents and my sister... thank you from the bottom of my heart for always believing in me and pushing me to be the man I am today. My mother is the rock of the family and by far the strongest of us all. She has a gift of making you feel invincible after you've had a conversation with her. No matter how big or crazy my dreams have been she has always ended the conversation with, "you can do it". Mom I love you, thank you. The wisdom of the family is my dad. So many lessons that I've never learned in school was taught to me by my dad. He has molded me into the loving and caring man that I strive to be each day. Dad, thank you and love you my man. My sister, is extremely determined. She has always been by my side right, wrong, or different. Necy, thank you for loving me and always being there for me.

The Pannell, Brooks, and extended family it's far too many for me to thank you individually. But although not mentioned in this book, the memories and experiences will always be there. Thank you for serving as an extension of my parents for guidance and love. From the bottom of my heart I truly thank you.

To my colleagues, managers, and mentors I want to take the time to thank you as well. Similar, to my extended family it's way too many of you to mention individually. The problem that comes with networking and building relationships is that you will cast a net so big that it become difficult to keep up at times. That's why I'm so thankful for LinkedIn because it pretty much does this work for me. I've had so many experiences, good, bad, and ugly throughout my career. It's been my network that has gotten me through it all. There are unfortunately mean spirited people that you have to deal with in corporate America but I've been blessed majority of the time to have a network of people that are truly genuine. To you, I tip my cap and thank you for all that you have done for me. A big part of this book was written because of you and I hope that I have made you proud.

Lastly, but definitely not least. I want to thank Charlamagne Tha God. For many of you that may not know who he is, Charlamagne is a TV, Radio, and social media influencer. He is best known as a former host on the Wendy Williams show and now the popular The Breakfast Club morning show on Power 105.1 FM. He may never even hear about this book, but I want to thank him for his book called

Black Privilege. For an ordinary guy like me, from a small town in Bluefield, WV he gave me the courage and confidence to write this book. Bro, I love watching your show because of course the guest, news, and stories. But you add a message to the show for people like me that's dreaming and striving to reach their goals. I can't thank you enough for creating a spark in me that wasn't there before I read your book.

ABOUT THE AUTHOR

Eric Pannell is an author, entrepreneur, and founder of several companies, including Startups With No Code (www.startupswithnocode.com) where he helps people to build a thriving business without any technical skills. He has been featured on Product Hunt, BetaList, and other popular magazines. Eric has a passion for helping others to achieve their goals and dreams through building a side hustle or a sustainable full-time business. He has over 14+ years of experience in the IT Project Management arena, leading projects upwards of $6M+ in budget. If you want to connect with Eric and talk about Project Management hop over to www.ericpannell.co

TO LEARN MORE ABOUT ERIC, GO TO:

www.startupswithnocode.com

www.ericpannell.co